Who Owns A River?

A Story of Environmental Action

by Wendy Wriston Adamson

Dillon Press, Inc.

Dillon Press, Inc., 500 South Third Street
Minneapolis, Minnesota 55415

Printed in the United States of America

Library of Congress Cataloging in Publication Data

Adamson, Wendy Wriston.
Who owns a river?

Bibliography: p. 94
SUMMARY: Traces the history of the St. Croix River in Minnesota and Wisconsin, the pollution of the river, and steps taken to save it.
1. St. Croix River, Minn. and Wis.—Juvenile literature. 2. Environmental protection—St. Croix River, Minn. and Wis.—Juvenile literature.
[1. St. Croix River, Minn. and Wis. 2. Environmental protection—St. Croix River, Minn. and Wis.] I. Title.
GB1225.M6A32 333.9'162'097751 76-53011
ISBN 0-87518-140-6

CONTENTS

These photographs are reproduced through the courtesy of the Minneapolis Public Library Bromley Collection; Minnesota Department of Economic Development; Walter H. Wettschreck, Minnesota Department of Natural Resources; Wisconsin Department of Natural Resources; Northern States Power Company; *Water Atlas of the United States,* by Geraghty, Miller, van der Leeden, and Troise, copyright 1973, Water Information Center, Inc.

INTRODUCTION

Growing up on the St. Croix River gave Bill, Dick, and David Stout opportunities many American youngsters never have. The oldest of the brothers was twelve when, in 1954, they moved to their home, about one hundred and fifty yards from the river bank and one-half mile downstream from where the Allen S. King power plant now stands. The boys swam, fished, water skied, and canoed on the river. When they were young, their parents would ferry them across to the Wisconsin shore in the evening, taking a tent, sleeping bags, food, and a flashlight, and then pick them up the following morning. As they grew older, they took longer canoe trips on their own along the St. Croix.

The Stout family remembers a scoutmaster who lashed

telephone poles together into a raft, constructed a tiny shelter on it, and took a local scout troop down the river to the Mississippi one summer. The brothers and their parents watched every year as thousands of geese flew up and down the river in the spring and fall on their annual migration. One year they saw a magnificent flock of whistling swans fly over. In the winter deer would occasionally cross the frozen river near their home. Upstream where the electric power plant was later built, low trees and bushes surrounded a lovely lagoon, full of wildlife. Often after dinner one of the Stout brothers would canoe upstream at dusk with Smudge, their black Labrador retriever, and watch the ducks swim among the reeds.

Life on the river was uneventful, and excitement came in unexpected ways. Three or four times, in years which had late springs, the Stouts and their neighbors saw a huge icebreaker come up the river, bringing in coal for the state prison or the power plant. The noise made by the boat and the breaking ice was deafening. During some springs flooding forced many of their friends from their homes.

Now the three Stout brothers have grown up, married, and had children of their own. They all still live near the St. Croix, and a third generation is learning to love it. Not much has changed. A coal barge now goes up the river each day to the power plant. Traffic on the river is much heavier, and hundreds of boats pass the house on a typical July weekend. But on a summer evening there are still parents who bundle their kids into a small runabout, tent and sleeping bags in tow, and drop them off for a night of camping. The kids can sit by a tiny fire and watch the moon reflecting on the water and know that because places like the St. Croix exist, they have learned what beauty is.

The St. Croix is a river loved and protected by those living along its banks, as well as those who visit during all seasons of the year. Its past flows through the veins of many of the valley families who have for generations lived along its cool waters. Who owns the river? Who owns any river? As "civilization" proceeds at its own frantic pace in the world, who is to speak for the river? As we shall see, many will.

The voices of those who have sat by a tiny campfire along its banks will be heard. We shall hear from those who have silently paddled a canoe on the water near Bayport in the early morning, watching the fog creep away. We shall listen to those who have maneuvered a kayak through the rapids near Riverside on a chilly day in May. We shall listen to men and women whose grandparents fished in the river's bays and inlets years ago. And we shall hear the children who still, in the Huck Finn tradition, pole downriver a few miles on a makeshift raft.

We own the river. You and I. What becomes of it depends on us.

The beautiful St. Croix is a historic river. People have lived on its banks for two thousand years.

1.

THE ST. CROIX VALLEY

As long as two thousand years ago, the people of the Dakota Indian nation canoed on the St. Croix River. Prehistoric mounds, villages, campsites, and burial grounds have been uncovered, and they tell a rich tale of life along the river valley. At that time the St. Croix was an area full of wildlife and wild rice. The Dakotas lived in harmony with nature, respected their surrounding environment, and never abused or wasted it.

Living as hunters and gatherers, the Dakota people, later to be called the Sioux, used the raw materials supplied by nature for survival. In the spring they made sugar from the maple trees; during the summer they picked wild strawberries and did some gardening; in the fall they harvested wild rice. Fish, birds, game, and wild rice provided a good diet. The Dakotas never hunted just for sport—they used skins from the animals they killed for clothing and shelter. Their canoes were made from birch bark and patched with pine gum.

In the 1600s another Indian tribe appeared on the scene. The Chippewas, or Ojibways, had been driven from their lands in the St. Lawrence Valley by the Iroquois, and had traveled west searching for a place to settle. They arrived carrying weapons of the white people, such as steel knives, guns, and gun powder, and with knowledge of warfare they had gained in battles in the east. The Dakotas were not prepared to cope with these sophisticated tools of "civilization." For the next two hundred years the tribes would fight occasional battles and then live for periods of time under uneasy truces. In 1745 the Chippewas drove out most of the Dakotas from the lower St. Croix Valley, but Dakota raids into the area continued into the middle of the nineteenth century.

The White People Arrive

The French explorer Daniel Greysolon, Sieur du Luth, is believed to have been the first white person to enter the St. Croix Valley, in 1680, although some historians suspect that Samuel de Champlain might have visited the area earlier. The canoe route from Lake Superior, twenty miles upstream along the Bois Brulé River, and then across the two-mile portage and downstream on the St. Croix to the Mississippi, had been well used by the Indians. Although the St. Croix has had other names such as Rivière du Tombeau and Rivière de la Madeleine, historians believe that its present name was given by the trader and explorer Nicolas Perrot, who called it

Rivière de Sainte-Croix. He probably named the river after another French explorer, Sainte-Croix, whose boat was wrecked near the place where the St. Croix joins the Mississippi River.

The white people immediately began to develop and use the St. Croix Valley. At first the most accessible and sought-after natural resource of the area was the beaver. There was a great demand for beaver pelts in Europe, where hats made of the fur were considered to be very fashionable. An extensive fur trade developed over the area of central North America, and the St. Croix Valley and surrounding countryside had a good share of the animals.

The Europeans depended on the Indians to do the actual trapping and skinning of the animals. If the Indians lived close to one of the many fur trading posts built by France and England, they would deliver the pelts directly there. They were paid in goods from Europe including guns, steel knives, liquor, axes, blankets, and even trinkets. Often they were paid very poorly and even cheated. Most of the actual trading, however, was done by the voyageurs, men who ventured in canoes out into the wilderness where the Indians lived. They would carry in goods from Europe, and carry out the beaver pelts.

The Voyageurs

The voyageurs were an unusual group of men, known for their incredible strength, endurance, and good humor in the face of great hardship. Most of them were French or French-Canadian. They thought nothing of canoeing for fifteen hours a day, and this was not at the leisurely pace many of us like to take on a Sunday afternoon on the river. They cooked their meals over the campfires and often had the energy to sing songs and spin tales late into the evening.

In her book, *The Voyageur,* Grace Lee Nute quotes Thomas L. McKenney as he describes these men:

> I can liken them to nothing but their own ponies. They are short, thick set, and active, and never tire. A Canadian, if born to be a labourer, deems himself to be very unfortunate if he should chance to grow over five feet five or six inches; and if he shall reach five feet ten or eleven, it forever excludes him from the privilege of becoming a voyageur. There is no room for the legs of such people in these canoes. But if he shall stop growing at about five feet four inches, and be gifted with a good voice, and lungs that never tire, he is considered as having been born under a most favourable star.[1]

There were two groups of voyageurs. The "pork eaters" canoed into the wilderness in the spring, exchanged goods, and returned with furs to Montreal or Quebec in the fall. They got their name because their traveling diet included a daily ration of bacon or pork. The "hivernants" or "winterers" were those who remained in the wilderness during the frigid winters to trade with the Indians.

Some of the voyageurs' birch bark canoes were large and sturdy enough for fourteen men and three tons of goods, and could travel on such rough, dangerous bodies of water as Lake Superior. The men were proud of their canoes, and here is a song they often sang about them:

My Birch-Bark Canoe

In my birch-bark, canoeing, in the cool of evening I ride
Where I have braved every tempest, St. Lawrence's rolling tide.

My canoe's of bark, light as a feather
That is stripped from silvery birch;
And the seams with roots sewn together,
The paddles white made of birch.

I take my canoe, send it chasing
All the rapids and billows acrost;
There so swiftly see it go racing,
And it never the current has lost.

It's when I come on the portage, I take my canoe on my back
Set it on my head topsy-turvy; it's my cabin too for the night.

— You are my voyageur companion! —
I'll gladly die within my canoe.
And on the grave beside the canyon
You'll overturn my canoe.[2]

The St. Croix-Bois Brulé riverway became a major route for the voyageurs. There was a French fur trading post on Madeline Island in Lake Superior, and another on the Mississippi River near the end of the St. Croix. Thousands of pelts were taken out of the St. Croix Valley and surrounding areas. At this time no one considered what the environmental effect of the fur trade might be. Beavers, in their capacity as dam builders, were the only force in nature to dam up running waters and eventually develop ponds and marshes. Such areas are important for a number of reasons, such as purifying and storing water and providing habitats, or living areas, for certain kinds of wildlife. The loss of such "beaver power" made a radical difference in the landscape.

In 1816 the U.S. Congress passed a law limiting fur trading to U.S. citizens, and coupled with the rapid drop in the beaver population, this caused the eventual death of any further major fur trade. The beaver population was never again to reach significant numbers.

Lumbering

Not much later, in the 1830s, another resource of the valley came to the attention of the white people. Magnificent forests of white pine stretched for miles on either side of the St. Croix. Just as important as the wood itself was a form of transportation for getting it to markets. The river, flowing as it did through these miles of magnificent forest, offered a paradise to the lumber industry.

In 1837 the Chippewa signed a treaty giving up their rights to huge areas of land along the river, and the whites moved in to lumber the valley. By agreement with the government they were first allowed to cut trees from a one-mile strip on the east bank and a three-mile strip on the west bank of the St. Croix.

The first lumber mill on the river was at Marine, and by 1855 there were seventeen mills from St. Croix Falls to Prescott. In 1847, before the industry was in full swing, English landscape artist Henry Lewis traveled the river and wrote, "the pine forests along the St. Croix are no longer equalled on the entire continent except along the Penobscot and Kennebec in Maine." These were enormous, stately white pines. The big trees cut in 1879 stood an average of 176 feet tall.

The piney banks of the St. Croix and many of its tributaries were stripped by about 1910. Often even the areas not suitable for cutting, or already cleared of any good lumber, were burned off and left in charry ruins. As a result, there is almost no virgin pine left along the river, except on steep hills or cliffs where the trees could not be reached. A glimpse of these few handsome trees today can give us some idea of the original beauty of the river valley.

Life in the Lumber Camps

The life of the loggers was often as hard and sometimes as colorful as that of the voyageurs. Thousands of settlers from such places as Maine, New York, Canada and even Switzerland—where many of them had previous experience cutting timber—arrived in the St. Croix Valley. The wood they were to cut would be used to build homes and other buildings all across the Midwestern United States.

The lumberjacks lived in logging camps in barracks-like cabins, usually without their families. Because they lived at such close quarters, they were not allowed to drink, and had to be in bed with the lights out by 9:00 P.M. six days a week. During the winter, when most water was frozen and washing themselves or their clothes was almost impossible, the aroma in the cabins was overwhelming. Even when they did wash their clothes the smell was terrible. Did you ever smell wet wool drying over a fire?

The loggers ate enormous breakfasts of flapjacks, cereals, ham, bacon, fried potatoes, and muffins. Dinners consisted of meat, potatoes, vegetables, and big desserts, while lunch was eaten out in the forest. Their hearty appetites were understandable considering the long hours of physical labor in the Minnesota and Wisconsin outdoors.

These hardy men in red shirts worked every hour of sunlight, and some of moonlight, cutting wood at least twelve hours a day. Throughout the late fall, winter, and early spring, when the river was frozen, they labored to cut as much wood as possible. They marked it with their brand, skidded it down to the river on huge horse-drawn sleds, and moved it onto the ice. Then, in the spring when

Living quarters in a logging camp. There wasn't much time for reading with lights out at 9 o'clock.

the ice melted, the great drive downriver would begin.

The logs moved best when the river was still high from the melted winter snows. Later in the summer the river was often too low to float them. In fact, the lumberjacks had an expression, "Low water, rusty saws." The branded logs would float down to a "boom" or barrier of connected floating logs that stretched across the river. There the boom company would sort the logs according to their ownership, measure them, and lash them into rafts to continue their float down the river. The big boom on the St. Croix was at Boomsite Park, just above Stillwater. More than 15.5 billion feet of logs went over it during the lumber years that ended around 1914.

Some log marks for lumber. Similar to cattle brands, each lumber company had its own, registered with the state of Minnesota or Wisconsin.

David Tozer	Thomas Carmichael	T. B. Walker
Pitchfork	Snowshoe	TWB

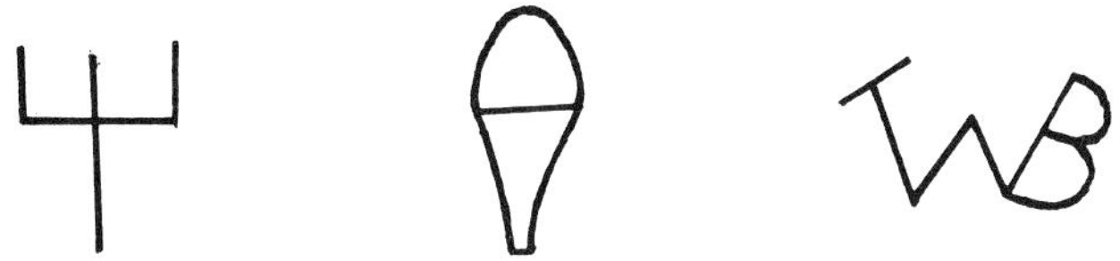

3

Log jams were a constant threat and were usually caused by low water. In 1883 a jam lasting fifty-seven days prevented all logs from passing through the area just below Taylors Falls. It often took hundreds of men and a number of boats to break up a jam, and some of the jams became big tourist attractions, bringing people from hundreds of miles away.

The loggers did their share of singing and partying, especially after paydays, which did not come too often. One of their songs goes:

I'm from the town of Bangor
  Down in the State of Maine,
A native American Irishman,
  That spakes the English plain;
I landed in Stillwater town
  In the year of fifty-three,
Me arm was strong, me heart was warm,
  And me courage bould and free![4]

The lumber era ended as abruptly as it began. No real program of reforestation had assured a continuing supply of wood. Selective cutting, which would have protected the young, unharvestable trees, had not been practiced. The land was ravaged, causing considerable erosion of the soil into the St. Croix. The lumber companies soon abandoned the area and the workers turned to farming, or migrated to the Pacific northwest to find more work. The white people had taken everything they could from the earth, with little regard for the consequences of such devastation. When profits were no longer forthcoming, they had gone elsewhere in search of new wealth. They had left the St. Croix Valley a sadly changed environment.

The Paddlewheelers

The only other "industry" on the St. Croix was the riverboats, called paddlewheelers, which ran on the river from 1838 to 1916. Many Swedes, Norwegians, and other new settlers arrived in the valley on these boats. Carrying mail and manufactured goods, the steamers served as a means of communication with the outside world. Imagine how exciting it must have been to see the first boat able to cut through the ice in the spring, bringing news six months old and long-awaited foods and materials from the east and Europe!

There was spirited competition for passengers on these colorful boats, and thousands of residents of the valley and the nearby Twin Cities enjoyed many a ride along the St. Croix. Tom Ellerbe, who still has a cabin on the river, remembers riding out from the metropolitan area for summer vacations when he was a boy:

> It was nearly seventy-five years ago. We would leave the dock in St. Paul and ride one of those steamers we called 'packets' down the Mississippi and then up the St. Croix. When we arrived at

A nineteenth-century paddlewheeler docking at Stillwater on the St. Croix.

Prescott the dock would be crowded with welcomers—including lots of small boys eager to help carry luggage or other cargo to any destination. We would leave a note with the Captain telling him on what day to stop and pick us up for the return trip home.

These boats even engaged in races on the river! Unfortunately for those who enjoyed them, the paddle-wheelers were not a very profitable business, and new forms of transportation eventually put them out of operation.

Farming

Farming became increasingly important along the river during the later nineteenth and early twentieth centuries. The closeness to the river and thus transportation of goods to markets meant a thriving business for wheat farmers. Many of these farms still operate today, because this is an area of rich soils, abundant water, and plenty of sunshine.

2.

A PORTRAIT OF THE RIVER

In the cool woods of northwestern Wisconsin, near the village of Solon Springs, a clear spring bubbles up out of the earth. Starting in a trickle, the spring water flows over the forest carpet and heads south to a pond. Out of the pond, in turn, flows a narrow stream which is the beginning of the St. Croix River.

All rivers must have a beginning, and many of the mightiest and most beautiful in the world originate in just such a modest manner, with spring water rushing out of the ground. The source, or upper region of a stream or river, is referred to as the headwaters. From its headwaters the St. Croix flows 165 miles southwestward to Prescott, Wisconsin, where it joins the Mississippi River on its way down to the Gulf of Mexico. As the St. Croix

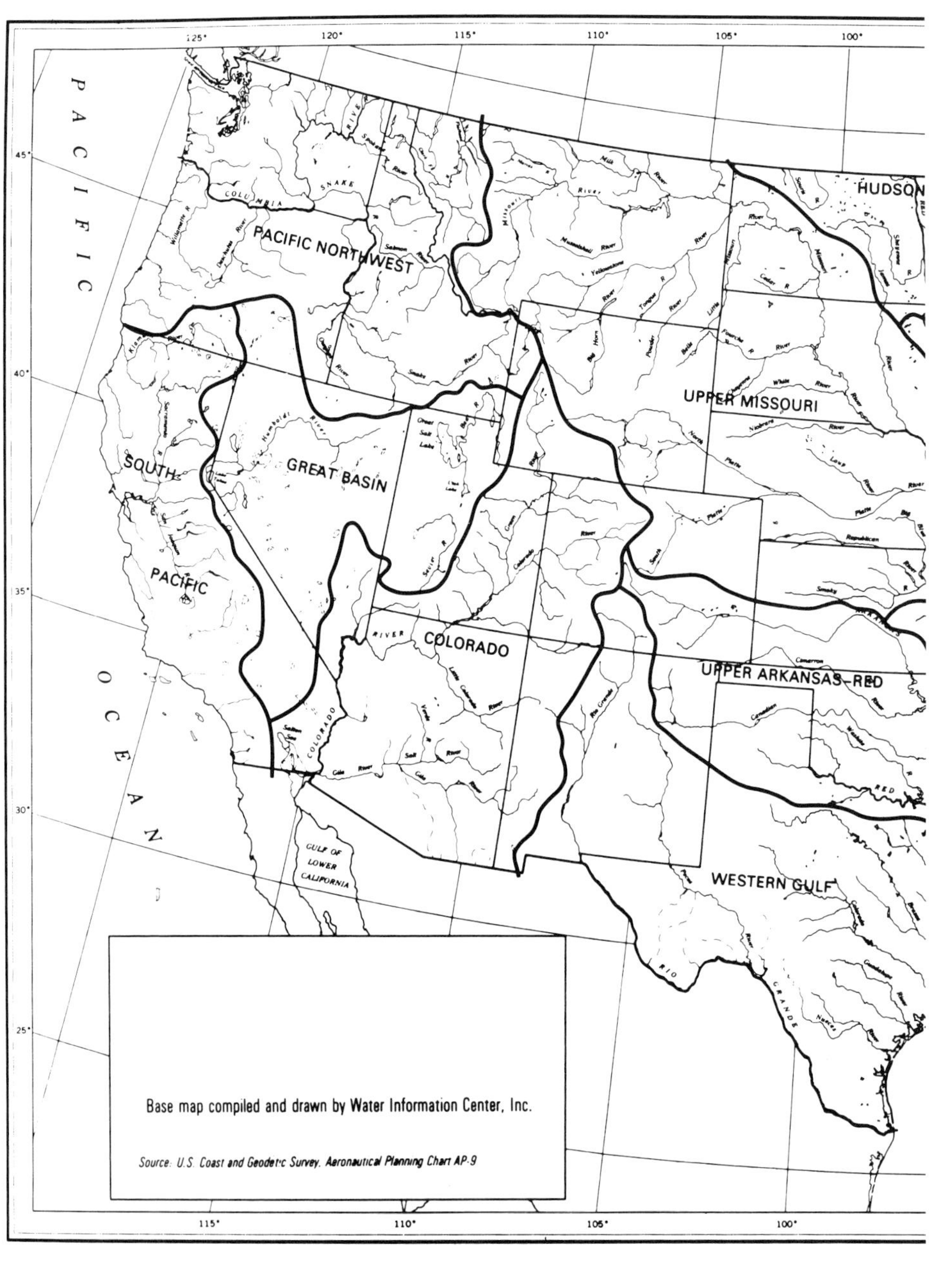

PACIFIC OCEAN
PACIFIC NORTHWEST
GREAT BASIN
SOUTH PACIFIC
COLORADO
UPPER MISSOURI
UPPER ARKANSAS–RED
WESTERN GULF
HUDSON
GULF OF LOWER CALIFORNIA
Base map compiled and drawn by Water Information Center, Inc.
Source: U.S. Coast and Geodetic Survey, Aeronautical Planning Chart AP-9

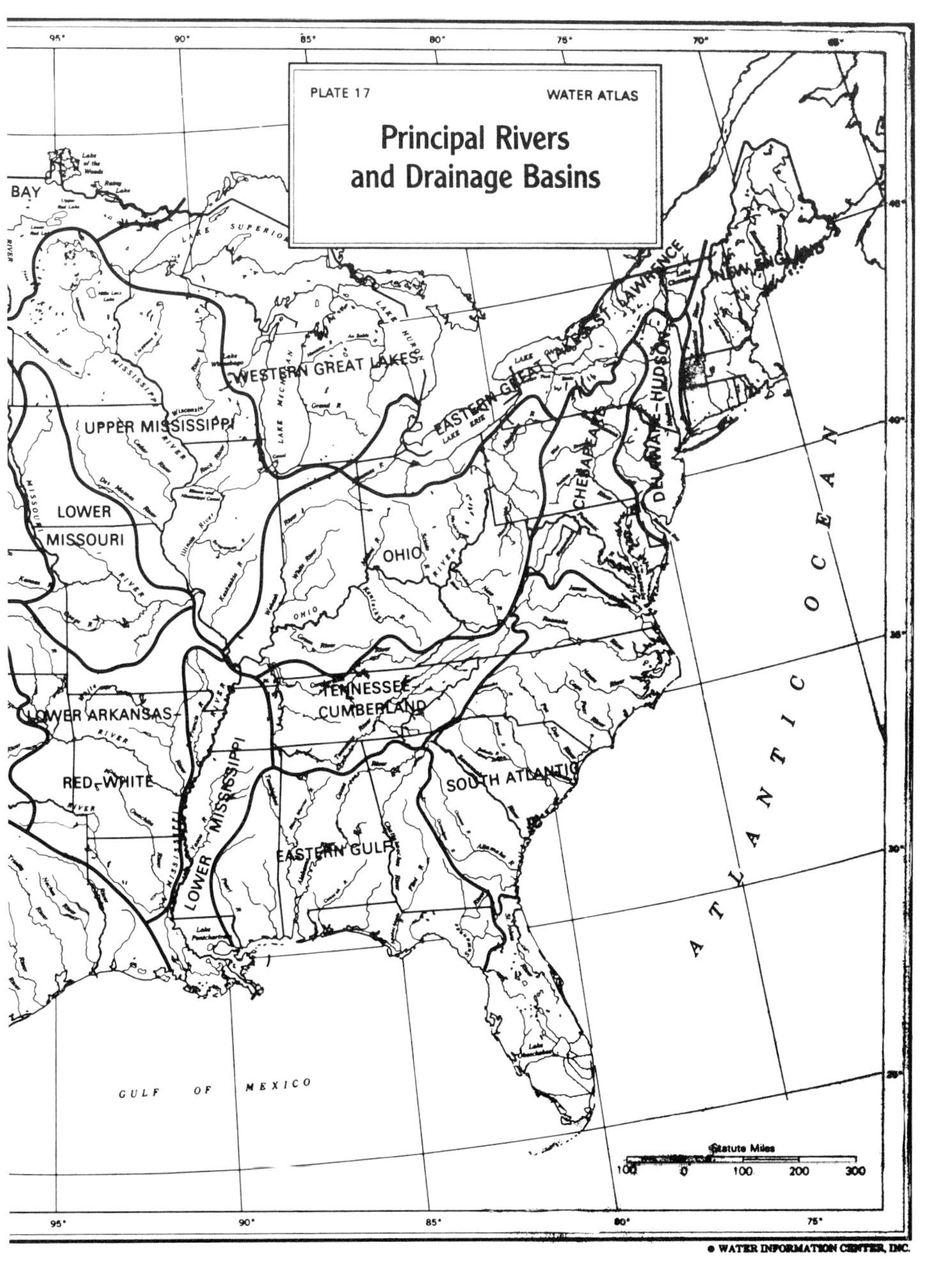
PLATE 17
WATER ATLAS
Principal Rivers and Drainage Basins
WESTERN GREAT LAKES
EASTERN GREAT LAKES
ST. LAWRENCE
NEW ENGLAND
HUDSON
DELAWARE
CHESAPEAKE
UPPER MISSISSIPPI
LOWER MISSOURI
OHIO
TENNESSEE CUMBERLAND
LOWER ARKANSAS
RED-WHITE
LOWER MISSISSIPPI
EASTERN GULF
SOUTH ATLANTIC
BAY
ATLANTIC OCEAN
GULF OF MEXICO
LAKE SUPERIOR
LAKE MICHIGAN
LAKE HURON
LAKE ERIE
Statute Miles
100 0 100 200 300
95°
90°
85°
80°
75°
70°

flows toward the Mississippi, it is fed by many other smaller rivers and streams, such as the Namekegon, Yellow, Apple, Kettle, and Willow Rivers. These tributaries are in turn fed by even smaller streams, and each of them has its own source, perhaps a spring or lake. The St. Croix itself is a tributary of the Mississippi River.

This network system of brooks, streams, lakes, ponds, and even springs is all part of the St. Croix watershed or drainage basin, which occupies an area of 7,760 square miles. A watershed is the entire area drained by a particular river and all its tributaries, or by a lake. The North American continent is divided into nine major watersheds, and the St. Croix watershed is actually a part of an even larger one, the Mississippi River watershed. In the United States alone there are some 3.25 million miles of rivers, all of which belong to one of these watersheds.

Millions of years ago, when great glaciers moved down from the north to cover much of this continent, two giant fault zones extending south from the area which is now Lake Superior guided "tongues" or "arms" of the glacier into the area which is now the St. Croix Basin. When the ice receded, the St. Croix Valley, which had been gouged out by the ice sheets, became a spillover area for Lake Superior. As the pressure of the heavy ice lessened, however, the crust of the earth rose enough along what is now Lake Superior's south shore to divide the lake from the St. Croix Basin. The high point of that rise is located near Solon Springs where the St. Croix begins flowing south, while just two miles away the Bois Brulé River flows northward.

The slope of a river (the amount it falls within a given distance) is called the gradient. The gradient of the St. Croix is considered to be fairly steep, because in 165 miles it falls 341 feet, or about 2 feet per mile. Its upper 38 miles is entirely in the state of Wisconsin, while the lower 127-mile stretch forms the Minnesota-Wisconsin boundary.

The entire St. Croix Valley was within the Wisconsin Territory when the lumber boom began in the middle of the last century. During the 1840s there was much controversy over whether the area west of the river, extending to the Mississippi River, should belong to Minnesota or Wisconsin. In 1848 the federal government made the river the western boundary of Wisconsin, and in the next year Minnesota was designated a territory with the St. Croix as its eastern border. Many residents of the valley had wanted the river to be under the authority of one territory or the other, and most preferred Minnesota, according to historical records. Their lobbying in Washington, however, was unsuccessful. As we shall see when we deal with some of the environmental aspects of the river, this division was to cause problems for future generations.

The Many Faces of the St. Croix

Depending on which part we look at, the St. Croix has several distinct personalities. The stretch of the river commonly referred to as the "upper St. Croix," which extends from the headwaters down to Taylors Falls on the west bank and St. Croix Falls on the east, is a narrow, clear-running body of water, fairly shallow and accessible only to canoes and very small flat-bottomed boats. The shoreline is relatively wild and rugged and has no startling elevations.

Just below the twin falls is the "lower St. Croix," beginning with the Dalles, a short, narrow stretch of

The river widens below the Dalles. Farther downstream it forms Lake St. Croix.

rushing waters bordered on both sides by high, rocky cliffs. This area was so named by French explorers because the high, slablike walls, at places rising more than one hundred feet from the water's edge, resembled the enormous paving blocks, called *dalles*, used in the construction of French cathedrals.

Below the Dalles the river widens as it flows down to Stillwater, where it is wide enough to be called "Lake St. Croix" although it is not, technically, a lake. At one point here it reaches its maximum width of twelve hundred feet. Along the banks we can see some clusters of buildings, including some heavy development around towns. While the upper St. Croix banks were mostly sandy, in the lower portion there is a good deal of rich farmland.

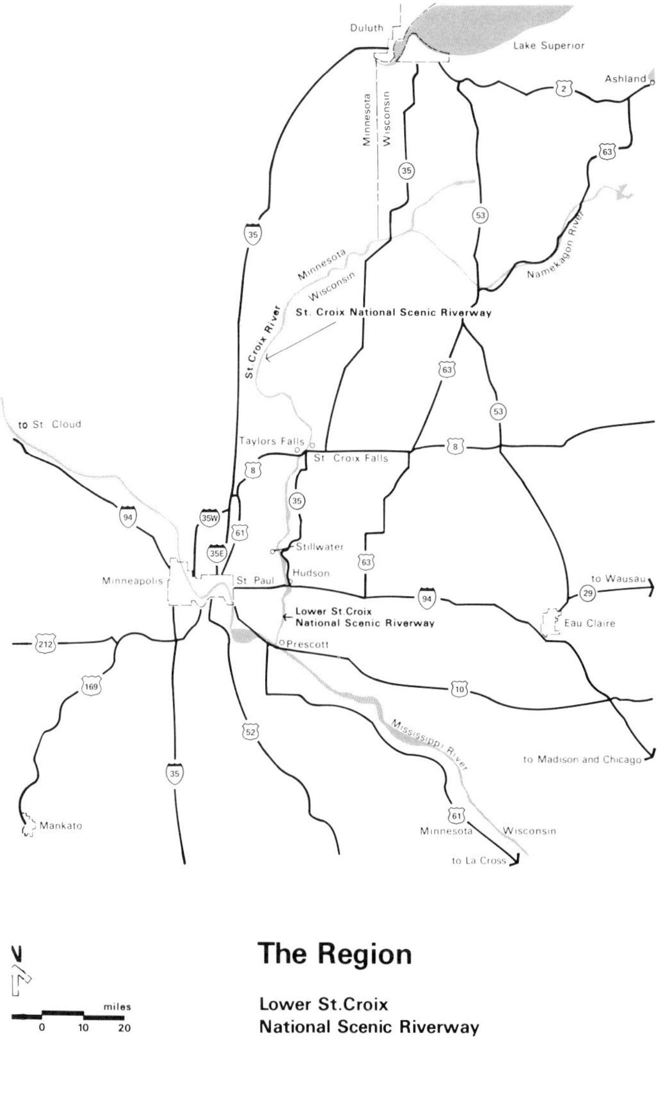

Duluth
Lake Superior
Ashland
Minnesota
Wisconsin
2
63
35
53
Namekagon River
35
Minnesota
Wisconsin
St. Croix River
St. Croix National Scenic Riverway
63
53
to St. Cloud
Taylors Falls
St. Croix Falls
8
8
94
35W
61
35
Stillwater
35E
63
Minneapolis
St. Paul
Hudson
to Wausau
29
94
Lower St.Croix
National Scenic Riverway
Eau Claire
212
Prescott
169
10
Mississippi River
52
to Madison and Chicago
35
61
Mankato
Minnesota
Wisconsin
to La Cross

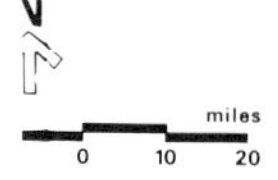

The Region

Lower St.Croix
National Scenic Riverway

The St. Croix changes not only according to where you are, but when you are there. Minnesota and Wisconsin, with hot summers and cold winters (temperattures are often twenty to thirty degrees below zero), have both extremes of climate. The river forms a crust of ice in the winter thick enough to support the cars and ice fishing houses which dot the landscape. In the spring that pleasant, quiet upper St. Croix becomes one of the most exciting whitewater areas in the Midwest, as melted snow and ice pour into its waters. But by the middle of the summer this same rushing river is subdued, and in many places too shallow for all but canoes. Even the rapids show just slight ripples as the waters pass quietly over and around boulders and rocks.

Life Along the River

At one time forests of gigantic white pine lined the banks of the river. Now we find a combination of deciduous, or hardwood, and evergreen trees, including white birch, oak, aspen, sugar maple, elm, and some white cedar, tamarack, and spruce. Once in a while a patch of white pine the loggers were not able to reach reminds us of the magnificence of the countryside before humans made their mark.

Living near the river are deer, waterfowl, upland game birds, and occasionally one can see a moose or bear. In the river and its tributaries are trout, sturgeon, muskellunge and smallmouth bass. It has been estimated that dozens of varieties of fish are found in the river and it is still one of the best fishing rivers in the Midwest. The St. Croix is also one of the few areas in the United States where a bald eagle can be seen regularly.

The fact remains that after all the description, the St.

Overlooking the St. Croix Valley from the Dalles, a lone sightseer looks down the river in the 1860s.

Croix is just a river like many other rivers in America. It is not particularly long, swift, or deep. It is not as breathtaking as many of those in the west, or as historical as some in the east. But it is unique in many ways.

It is one of the cleanest rivers of its size in the Midwest. It is fed by clear, sparkling trout brooks and bass streams. Although some portions of it are wild and rugged, it is only one-half hour away from a major metropolitan area, Minneapolis and St. Paul, Minnesota, with a population of nearly two million people. It is largely unspoiled and undeveloped, a fact made remarkable by that closeness to civilization.

3.

THE ALLEN S. KING PLANT

Sometimes polluters, or would-be polluters, do the environment a service by drawing the attention of the public to a great natural resource that has been taken for granted in the past. Often it is just one proposed power plant, or one planned dam, which can light the spark of an environmental awareness and serve to mobilize the citizens in their efforts to protect and wisely use a natural resource. The Allen S. King power plant served just such a purpose on the St. Croix.

On May 6, 1964, the Northern States Power Company (NSP), which supplies electricity to most of Minnesota and parts of Wisconsin and North and South Dakota, announced plans to construct and operate a 550,000 kilowatt coal-burning electric power plant on land they

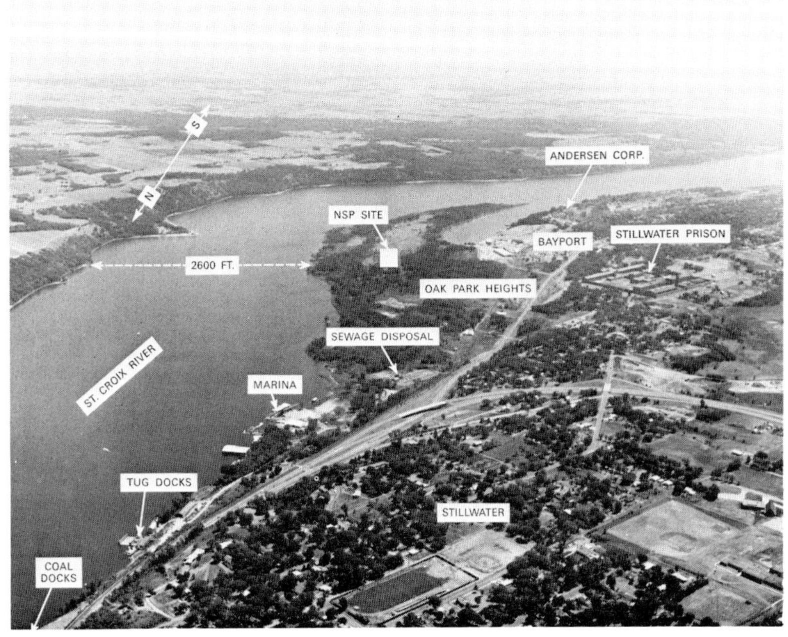

The Northern States Power Company site of the Allen S. King power plant. This picture was taken shortly before the power plant was built on the St. Croix.

had owned since the 1940s at the tiny community of Oak Park Heights on the St. Croix River. They also said that they would build a second, larger unit with a capacity of 750,000 kilowatts on the same site at a later date.

Before construction could begin, they had to secure permission from: (1) the Minnesota Conservation Commission, which had authority over the taking of water from any river, lake, stream, or pond in the state; (2) the Minnesota Water Pollution Control Commission, which had authority over discharges into any river, lake, stream, or pond in the state; (3) the U.S. Army Corps of Engineers, which had authority over navigation and docking on the river (barges would transport coal up the St. Croix to the plant), and (4) the Village of Oak Park Heights, which had authority over zoning.

NSP expected these permits to be secured within a few months, and construction would follow as soon as possible. Most business people and chambers of commerce in the Washington County area around Oak Park Heights supported the plant, as did most governmental units. After all, it would bring jobs which would contribute millions of dollars to the local economy. Estimates were $7 million in construction wages and $500,000 per year for operation. Also, the enormous property taxes that the company would pay on the plant would benefit the community.

Opposition Develops

But opposition developed immediately, centered around an organization called "Save the St. Croix, Inc." This group was made up primarily of Minnesota and Wisconsin citizens who lived on or used the river. It began with a few hundred members and grew to a coalition of twenty-six organizations with more than thirty thousand members, plus an additional ten thousand signers of petitions against the King plant. Their objections were many. Northern States Power had announced the building of the plant without consulting the citizens living on the river, and with no apparent regard for their opinions. Environmental objections fell into several categories:

- Thermal Pollution. NSP estimated that the first unit would use 660 cubic feet of water per second to cool the power plant. This water would then be discharged back into the St. Croix at a temperature of ten to seventeen degrees higher than when it was removed. The amount of heat returned to the river would be equal to two thousand tons of coal burned per day, or the heat output of twenty thousand home heating furnaces going full blast. Because of the expense, NSP had no plans to build cooling towers that could cool the water considerably before returning it to the river.

Citizens were concerned that in the winter this heat would melt the ice, limit winter recreation, and create thin ice hazards. In the summer, when the water reaches very high temperatures because of the weather, this ten to seventeen degrees could raise the water to temperatures as high as eighty-four to ninety-nine degrees. Such high temperatures could kill fish and other animals and plants in the river, and could also cause an imbalance in plant growth.

• Barge Traffic. In order to supply coal to keep the King plant operating, barges would have to travel up the St. Croix carrying about 2 million tons of fuel a year. Weekly traffic estimates predicted three huge "tows" of fifteen barges each, or greater numbers of smaller tows going up and down the river. The prospect of barge traffic concerned the people who fished and boated on the river, as well as the parents of children who would be swimming in it. Anyone who had seen the St. Croix on a hot July afternoon knew how many chances of collision would exist.

• Air Pollution. Coal burning is one of the dirtiest ways to produce electricity. Nevertheless, coal is a very popular energy source in the United States, because we have an enormous supply of it. We probably have enough to power the country for two centuries if we are willing to indulge in strip mining to extract it from the earth and then to allow further pollution of the air. Burning coal gives off a number of pollutants, of which the most harmful is sulfur dioxide. New air quality standards in the country and in various states have somewhat restricted such pollution, and industry has developed methods of near-clean burning of coal. However, these involve expensive equipment, and many companies are unwilling to make the investment necessary to minimize emissions.

Sulfur dioxide is not only harmful to human health, but it also can cause severe damage to foliage, sometimes even killing trees. Citizens living in the lush, green valley of the St. Croix were concerned that emissions from the plant would damage the growth there and endanger the health of the people as well. Wisconsin citizens were upset because pollution generated in Minnesota would be blown across the St. Croix by the wind, which knows no boundaries.

• Visual Pollution. One of the ways in which NSP planned to reduce such air pollution was to build a smokestack so high that pollutants released into the air would be widely dispersed by winds. This is a known method of lessening air pollution in one location. However, it is not completely effective. Even if dispersed, the polluted air goes somewhere, and if it rains, sulfur gases can be converted to acids harmful to plants.

The high smokestack would introduce visual pollution into the valley. Not only would the plant itself present an image of ugliness, located on the beautiful banks of the river, but a smokestack six hundred to eight hundred feet high would tower over the valley and be visible for miles up and down the river. Even one such structure dominating this fairly flat, gently rolling valley would be enough to alter its character.

• Water Pollution (other than thermal). This was not one of the major concerns of the Save the St. Croix organization, because it was not anticipated to be one of the more serious environmental problems. However, there was the possibility of pollution from the barges using the river, and citizens were also alert to the possibility that the coal piles along the river could leach acids into the water.

The Threat of Industrialization

In addition to these specific areas of concern, citizens expressed some general objections to the building of the NSP plant along the St. Croix. One objection was often heard—since the Mississippi River, which originates in and flows through Minnesota, is already industrialized and polluted, why not build the plant there, where it would not be in such contrast to its environment?

This raised a complex issue. Is it a lesser evil to concentrate all ugliness, all pollution, in one area, when all citizens benefit from the products of such ugliness (in this case electricity)? The Mississippi River was once a beautiful, natural, clean river. It still is, for the most part, north of the Twin Cities. Should people living near its banks be continually subjected to more and more pollution on the grounds that it doesn't matter any more? There are some reasons why the answer might be yes. The water is already warmer from other industrial uses; fish life is already curtailed; smokestacks are a common sight on its banks, and not many people rely on this area of the Mississippi for quiet canoeing or fishing. Swimming in it is considered dangerous to your health.

Nevertheless, it was important that residents of a beautiful area such as the St. Croix Valley not say simply "the answer is to put this dirty plant somewhere else, away from our doorstep," without concern for the pollution it would cause elsewhere. They, too, should work for

The St. Croix and Mississippi rivers meet near Prescott, Wisconsin. Note the pollution in the Mississippi River.

close regulation of industry on the Mississippi so that that river might eventually be cleaned up. Too many of us think that if we cannot see the pollution from our summer cabin or our home, then all problems have been solved.

On the other hand, the citizens of the St. Croix realized that they had in their river one of the last few clean, lovely bodies of water in the country, and they wanted to maintain it in this condition so *all* could enjoy it. Behind their concern over this particular power plant was a larger concern over the future of the valley as a whole. They feared that the introduction of this plant would be just the first in a long string of industrial development along the river. Once one company got its foot in the door, it would be easier for the next one, and still easier for the next. They were determined that such industrialization would not take place.

The Northern States Power Company was quick to answer its critics. It claimed that thermal pollution would not be serious, that barge traffic would be minimal and confined mostly to weekdays, that air pollution equipment would keep emissions under control, and that the plant would benefit the valley in many ways, most of them economic. Another citizens' group was formed in support of NSP called "Share the St. Croix," and they insisted that the valley needed the plant. Scientists, lawyers, and concerned citizens testified at length in federal and state water pollution control hearings. Even though these hearings were concerned with the merit of proposed federal water pollution control legislation, and had no direct bearing on the outcome of the debate, they helped to clarify the issues involved.

The Political Side of the Question

The question of the Allen S. King plant made everyone more aware of environmental issues, and it also revealed areas where the law was inadequate. Senator Gaylord

Nelson said that the entire St. Croix debate was a "classic example of the inability of state and local governments to deal with interstate pollution problems." Not only did one state, one federal, and one local government unit have authority over the project, but another state was closely, if not legally, involved. At the proposed power plant site, half of the St. Croix water belongs to Wisconsin. All the negative effects would be felt just as heavily by Wisconsin citizens. They too would suffer if thermal pollution affected the fish population. They too would have to cope with the barge traffic, breathe the air from the plant, and swim in the water. And they would have to get up every morning and look across the river at huge piles of coal and a high smokestack. Nevertheless, since the plant would be built on the Minnesota side of the river, the people of Wisconsin were not to be consulted on any decision.

Protecting America's Rivers

Everyone soon came to realize that the issues they were debating were larger than just the NSP plant or even the St. Croix River. They were asking a question which was being heard all over America. How can we best use our political system to preserve and protect our land, and at the same time insure the rights of citizens to participate in making decisions which affect our environment? Nationally known conservationist Sigurd Olson said at this time:

> This is not purely a local issue. This is a national issue. We are concerned with city problems and recreational areas all over the country . . . One of the greatest challenges we have is keeping America beautiful, planning so that there will always be open space, and so that we can always say that this is the land we love

because it gives us opportunities not only to make a living, but the opportunity of a good life.[5]

It became increasingly clear that if individual villages and town governments could decide who could build and pollute on *their* land, then pollution would abound if the price tag was high enough. Even if some communities were environmentally aware and maintained high standards, the next community upriver could negate all their efforts. Many community governments simply are not strong enough to say "no" to the pressures of big industry and big money. Often they feel they need this money to build better schools, roads, and to develop other public services in their communities, and that these are fair tradeoffs for a little pollution.

Standardization of water quality laws was needed, not only in one area of one state, but all across the country. Water is not self-contained. All bodies of water are part of a larger system, and what causes pollution in one area may eventually cause harm in others. So while the citizens of the St. Croix Valley debated the issues on one power plant, similar debates were going on all over the country. One concept was consistently emerging—the federal government must take some responsibility for coordinating and regulating water use all over the United States.

4.

THE ECOLOGY OF RIVERS

Rivers and streams have a unique ecological system, far different from stable bodies of water such as lakes or ponds. Probably their most noticeable feature is constant motion. Rivers are always traveling, usually in one general direction, and this affects the life within them.

Not only is the water in a river always moving, but there are great differences in the speed of this movement. A stretch of water may be a slow, meandering section, a lake that is almost closed off from the rest of the river, a run of rapids and waterfalls, or quiet backwaters. One reason for this is the natural geological formation of the river valley. Water will tumble quickly down a hill or cliff, while it will wander more slowly across a wide, flat plain.

Rapids on the St. Croix River. Some river plants and animals prefer fast-moving water.

Plants and animals living underwater must constantly adapt to the movement of the waters. Sometimes they cling tightly to underwater rocks, while at other times they have to swim upstream most of the time just to stay in the same place, like Alice in Wonderland. This does not mean that a river is an unfriendly environment. Many plants and animals thrive under just such unstable conditions.

Spectacular waterfalls are one example of the many faces of a river.

Rivers and streams provide various habitats, or living areas, along any one section. Some habitats may consist of fast-moving water, rapids and riffles, while other habitats may be quiet, fairly stationary pools. River animals may live in more than one habitat. For instance, a trout may spend most of its time deep in a shady pool, move to another part of a stream for feeding, and use yet another area for spawning. A healthy stream needs certain conditions in order to sustain life: adequate nutrients or food (but not an overabundance, which can cause too much growth, choking the stream); sunlight (necessary for the process of photosynthesis); correct temperatures (warm enough for plants, cool enough for fish); unpolluted water, and an adequate oxygen supply. Most of these conditions are interdependent.

Seasonal changes in the level and width of a river can greatly disturb its ecology. Flooding usually happens during the spring thaw. When the snow melts, a gentle mountain stream can become a raging cascade of icy water. A heavy rainstorm can change a lazy river into a swollen and dangerous one. Such transformations can occur overnight. When faced with such unexpected force and violence, many animals and plants are ripped from their habitat and swept downstream. Sometimes they survive, but often, particularly in the case of plant life, they are destroyed.

River levels begin to drop in the spring when leaves come out along the banks. This occurs because of the process of transpiration in which trees drink up huge quantities of water through their roots and give it off through their leaf surfaces. Along the riverbank this water would have seeped into the river. Throughout the summer and fall, water levels continue to drop as normal evaporation occurs and sources of meltwater disappear. In late summer or early fall most rivers reach their low point. They may be reduced to a thin trickle of water or even a dry stream bed. In the southwestern part of the United States, many rivers and streams dry up completely for several months every year. Such drastic change causes serious disturbance and damage to the living things along and in the river.

Much vegetation is swept away by floods, and more is killed by the prolonged submersion. On the other hand, nothing that requires substantial water all through the year can survive along a stream which contains water for only six to nine months. Most rivers rarely experience such extremes in water level, but most do vary by a few feet during the year. If the banks of the river are steeply sloped, damage is usually minimal. But if the river is situated along a relatively flat plain, even a few feet can cause enormous damage. The flatter the terrain, the farther the water will spread during any flooding. Not only do floods damage homes and threaten plant and animal life, but they also cause serious erosion as they wash away irreplacable topsoil from the banks.

Another characteristic of rivers and streams is their constant mixing or turbulence. Waters toss, turn, pick up solids, and move them along downstream. They exert a force against any life in the water, which means that every spot along the river is constantly changing. Such changes are in sharp contrast to a lake, in which the plants and some animals can remain in the same spot for months.

Instability is the key word in describing rivers and streams, because these bodies of water are never inactive or dormant unless dried up. Instability causes hardships for living things both in and along the banks of these rivers, and yet many species of life thrive in just such a situation. Oxygen is needed by almost all animals and plants for survival, and the constant mixture and movement of the water enables it to capture large amounts of oxygen from the air. Thus streams are oxygen-rich bodies of water, while small lakes or ponds are often oxygen-poor, and cannot as easily support life.

Humans and Rivers: The Downstream Mentality

People can have a destructive effect on rivers and streams. If you dump a pollutant in the water in front of your cabin on a lake, where does it go? Not very far, unless the lake is very large, and so the next day when you want to go swimming, you think twice. Unfortunately, whatever you dump into a river travels downstream to your neighbors. Not only may they have no control over what you put into the river, but they may rely on the river for their drinking water, or for irrigating their crops, or for swimming or fishing. And yet, you, who live upstream, don't have to sacrifice any of these activities—unless someone upstream from you is also irresponsible.

The mentality of "what you can't see won't hurt you" has caused many pollution problems in this country, but rivers are uniquely designed to encourage such irresponsible thinking. Why should people in Minnesota worry about the quality of the drinking water in Louisiana? Why should industries worry about fishing or swimming downstream? Isn't our economy more important than catching a few fish on a Sunday afternoon?

Our Water Supply

The illusion has existed for centuries that we have on

this earth so much water that a little pollution of it here and there will simply be a drop in the ocean, and thus harmless. The facts tell us differently.

The total amount of water in the world has remained the same for millions of years. This water is constantly being reused and recycled as it moves through what we call the hydrological cycle. Water from open lakes, rivers, and oceans is evaporated by the heat of the sun. The water vapor then rises and is blown by wind over land masses. As it rises, it cools, and water droplets (rain, snow, or ice) are formed, which fall as precipitation back to earth. Then this water seeps into the ground, or it flows back to streams and rivers, again heading for the sea. A complete cycle can take hundreds of years. The water you use for your bath tonight may have been used for cooking by the Romans. But the total water supply has not actually increased or decreased during the process.

Our use of water, however, has increased enormously. In ancient villages, a person might have used as much as five gallons of water a day. Today a city dweller uses about one hundred fifty gallons a day in the United States, an amount which does not include industrial uses. Most of this increase has taken place during the last hundred years. While our population has a bit more than doubled since the turn of the century, we use more than four times as much water. Predictions are that in the United States we may be using close to all fresh water available in our lakes, streams and reservoirs by the end of the century. Water may be the "crisis" of the 1980s, as energy is in the 1970s.

What is disturbing is that we do not simply use water and then return it to the environment relatively unchanged. We alter it, pollute it, and return it to the hydrological cycle in such dirty form that it cannot be reused or purified by natural processes. Let us take a look at some of the biggest sources of such pollution.

A human must take in about 2½ quarts of water every day, in the form of beverages or food. In addition, uses of water include:

flushing a toilet	3 gallons
taking a bath	30 to 40 gallons
taking a shower	5 gallons per minute
washing dishes by hand	10 gallons
washing machine—1 load	30 gallons

According to the *World Book* "it takes up to 65,000 gallons of water to make a ton of steel, 10 gallons of water to refine a gallon of gasoline, 250 tons of water to produce a ton of paper and 300 gallons of water to make a barrel of beer."[6]

Industrial Pollution

Industry is the greatest polluter by far. Water is used in hundreds of industries in the United States, for such purposes as cooling, cleaning of materials, moving substances from one part of a plant to another, and diluting them. Rivers are an ideal source of water for industry. The water can be fed into the plant from a point slightly upstream, used, polluted, and dumped out downstream.

The substances released into the water are called effluents. Sometimes they are combined with water that was removed and used during a process, while at other times they are pure waste. Industrial effluents can be classified in several categories according to what damage they do to rivers and streams.

• Toxic substances. These are poisonous substances such as sulphuric acid, lead, and acids from mine wastes (especially run-off water from strip mines) which are deadly and can kill all life in a stream. Also included in this category are infectious, disease-causing substances, such as bacteria from a stockyard, and dangerous pesticides used by farmers along river banks.

- Substances causing undesirable effects. These may cause unpleasant colors, odors, or tastes, but they may not necessarily be dangerous.
- Easily broken down materials which upset the balance of life in the stream. We can all remember when it

Industries often pollute rivers by dumping their waste products into them. Here is a view of waste products from a chemical plant flowing into the Mississippi River.

became apparent a few years ago that the phosphates in laundry detergents were supplying too much nourishment to algae, which in turn grew so fast that they choked rivers and streams. This is an example of an overabundance of a seemingly harmless material that upset the ecological balance.

• Materials which break down very slowly, and thus use up stream oxygen. Some of these materials, such as cellulose from paper mills and oil, cloud the water, which hinders the entry of sunlight for photosynthesis. Also, they often smother life on the river bottom and damage the gills of fish.

• Heat. Thermal pollution can kill fish and other life by high temperatures, since their oxygen needs increase when water temperatures rise.

• Radioactive materials from nuclear power plants. These are a special kind of pollutant that requires thousands of years to become entirely harmless. They are released into rivers in seemingly minute, inconsequential amounts; for example, in the cooling water from nuclear reactors. As they are taken in by small fish or plants, which are then eaten by progressively larger and larger fish, they are concentrated in dangerous amounts; that is, dangerous to persons who eat such fish. The dumping of *any* radioactive material into the environment is an example of the worst kind of "downstream mentality." Not only may the people literally downstream from the power plant be exposed to harmful substances, but those in future generations may be severely affected. Exposure to radioactivity can cause genetic damage that results in birth defects or such diseases as leukemia in children of persons exposed.

When we examine these types of pollution, we must

remember that life in the rivers is extremely sensitive, and what may seem harmless to us is very harmful to river life. Often in the gills of fish and other stream creatures just one thin layer of cells separates the blood stream or interior fluids from the surrounding environment. Some chemicals can easily penetrate this thin layer and poison the internal system of the fish. Others are capable of clogging or doing damage to the gills, so that the fish eventually suffocates. Stream life is fragile when faced with the many poisons that we inflict upon it.

Sewage

Individuals do their share when it comes to contaminating rivers. Perhaps the single most widespread form of river pollution is the sewage which each household generates. Raw sewage contains all types of germs, not to mention undesirable odors. While most towns have sewage treatment systems, these are often inadequate. Many cottages and other small dwellings along rivers that were built in the earlier part of the century still dump directly into the river.

Another destructive function of sewage comes from its high nutrient content, primarily nitrogen, which provides an overabundance of food for algae. What results is a population explosion in which the algae take over the river. They grow so thickly that other forms of life cannot survive because they cannot compete for oxygen. The water becomes pea green in color, smells foul, and the absence of light and oxygen result in death for all living things. This process is called eutrophication.

While the most common answer to industrial pollution seems to be a combination of proper treatment and an end to dumping, at the present time there seems to be no alternative to dumping sewage into the nation's waterways. The millions of gallons of sewage generated daily in America—including toilet wastes, dishwater, laundry water, garbage from home disposal systems, and bath or shower water—must go somewhere. Fortunately we have devised some simple sewage treatment which can provide a screen of sorts between our homes and the river. There are three basic levels of treatment.

- Primary treatment consists simply of separating out some of the solids. This is usually done by screening and allowing materials to settle out in basins.
- Secondary treatment takes the effluent from the primary treatment process and oxidates it, using filters, aeration, oxidation ponds and other means. Oxidation is the process through which oxygen is added to water, and it removes taste-producing gases.
- Tertiary treatment takes the water from the secondary process and passes it through a fine sand filter, further removing contaminants.

In the best of such plants, which provide tertiary treatment, clean, chlorinated water is returned to the river to travel downstream to the next community. You can see the importance of such treatment when you consider that people on the lower end of the Mississippi sometimes drink water which has already been used by five or six people!

It is important to remember that these systems are able to deal only with normal household sewage. They cannot deal with motor oil, gasoline, paint, pesticides, and other dangerous substances that do not break down easily through natural processes. Many smaller communities in the United States have not yet built adequate sewage systems. Some systems perform only a partial treatment of the water, so that it is not completely clean when returned to rivers.

Erosion

When we speak of erosion, we normally think of the farmer whose topsoil is worn away by rain or wind, so that the land is not suitable for growing crops. However, erosion, or the wearing away of the soil, can happen anywhere with serious consequences. Anything which strips the land of its growth, whether grasses, trees, or brush, robs it of a protective coating of roots. Growing plants can absorb large amounts of rainwater which otherwise would wash away bare soil. Such growth can also hold the soil together, so that it is protected from harsh winds. When the ground cover along a river is destroyed, erosion occurs. Clear cutting by the lumber industry, in which all trees are removed at once, can cause severe erosion. Heavy grazing of livestock can also remove growth, as can improper farming practices. Construction of buildings or highways near a river removes plants and replaces them with cement, so that rainwater will run off quickly into the river, sometimes even carrying sections of a highway.

What is the result of such erosion on the river itself? When a rainstorm causes tons of dirt to be dumped into a river, the resulting cloudiness of the water robs it of the sunlight that most underground plants need to grow. When plant growth is inhibited, all animals in the river suffer the consequences of reduced supplies of food and oxygen. If the erosion is sufficiently heavy, the silt in the water can destroy animal life by clogging the gills. In addition, a heavy deposit of silt can completely cover and kill all bottom life. The stream becomes muddy, and continuing erosion will just make matters worse. Only if humans step in at this point and replant along river banks can a river's health be slowly restored.

Managing Rivers

We have destroyed rivers and streams not only by polluting them, but also by restructuring them. Dams, built for water power, controlling flood-prone rivers, or creating lakes, have wiped out more miles of stream and river than we can count. While some dams are certainly justified, too often in the past environmental considerations have been ignored.

Channelization is the process of dredging, clearing, and straightening creeks, streams, and rivers. Used for "flood control" and "improved irrigation of farmland," it has resulted in straight, sterile, fast-flowing gutters of silt and debris, devoid of life. The process of recreating nature has ruined thousands of streams in our country.

The instability of rivers makes their ecology extremely delicate. We have taken for granted that rivers will continue to flow clearly and beautifully forever, even if they are abused by those along their banks. Not so, because a river can even "die." It can become unfit for all life, and end up nothing more than an open, flowing sewer. It is possible to clean up polluted rivers, but it takes an enormous input of time, effort, and money, not to mention the cooperation of everyone living along their banks. The Willamette River in Oregon, for example, was cleaned up by a cooperative effort of citizens and government agencies. The easiest answer is not to pollute rivers in the first place.

5.

THE OUTCOME OF THE ALLEN S. KING DEBATE

The people of the St. Croix felt that their river was threatened by a number of the types of pollution we have just discussed, and a few others as well. The debate over the building of the Allen S. King plant continued into the spring of 1965. Hundreds of letters to the editors of local papers were published on both sides of the question. Early in the debate the *Stillwater Weekly Gazette* said that those opposing the plant were "unduly excited" and claimed in a headline, "Plant Won't Hurt the River: A Few Parties Want $60 Million NSP Plant Moved Elsewhere." In another editorial they asked, "Are year around jobs for hundreds of men and women more important to the St. Croix Valley than a few weeks of recreation?"

The Minneapolis and St. Paul papers were more

cautious. They both expressed concern for preserving the unique nature of the valley. At one point the *St. Paul Pioneer Press* made what many felt was a very constructive and fair suggestion—that NSP go ahead with the construction of another plant that was already planned in Red Wing, Minnesota, and allow more time for the St. Croix location to be discussed. NSP rejected the alternative offered by the St. Paul paper.

During this period NSP had repeatedly said that it must begin construction immediately to meet the state's future power needs. The concept of urgency is sometimes used by industries that wish to hurry a project through government and citizen review. However, if industry uses proper advance planning, there should not be any such last minute crises.

The national press was also very interested in the question, because it recognized that what happened to the St. Croix could affect what happened in many other such cases throughout the United States. The *New York Times,* the *Washington Post,* the *Nation,* and the *New Republic* all carried articles on the debate. A timely editorial in Life magazine expressed the reason for such concern:

> When does a local conservation issue become national? In a real sense the whole country suffers every time Americans make a bad choice, even a local one, that allows the needless waste of any of our natural treasures. The destruction of such resources is irrevocable; no one can pass that way again.[7]

The debate became political at times and even involved personal attacks. There were accusations that the Save the St. Croix organization was "stacked" with St. Paul citizens who wanted the plant built in *their* city so that they would receive the economic benefits. During the January 1965 federal water pollution control hearings,

Senator Gaylord Nelson, who was born and raised in Wisconsin, and Sigurd Olson, a well-known conservationist who lives in northern Minnesota, came to testify on the river. Both men had spent many years enjoying the wilderness of the St. Croix. Senator Nelson said during the hearings:

> During the past one hundred years we have wrought more wanton destruction of our landscape than any previous civilization accomplished in one thousand years. We now say, what a pity our ancestors didn't have the foresight to husband our bountiful resources more sensibly. How much richer we would be both in esthetic and material wealth had they had more vision and courage. Before this case is decided, I think we all should ask ourselves this question: "What are our great-grandchildren going to say about us a half a century from now?"[8]

Washington County Probate Judge John T. McDonough, a leader of the pro-plant forces, referred to Senator Nelson and Olson as intruders who had no business interfering. He described Senator Nelson as:

> . . . the knight on a white horse who galloped over here to tell us how to run our affairs. People of this valley resent the junior senator from the East galloping over here to tell us we're attempting to destroy the last clean river in the Midwest. People around here resent the implication of self styled conservationists that the NSP plant would spoil the river, and that what NSP plans to do is morally wrong.[9]

Personal differences aside, probably the most controversial statement made during the entire debate came from Judge McDonough. He said that public debates on such issues as the Allen S. King plant were useless because only public agencies could make the decisions called for, and they should be able to make them without pressure or influence from the citizens. Did the public have a voice in the resolution of the issue? Who should make the decision? As the laws were written, it was the responsibility of the four agencies mentioned earlier. But was the law adequate?

The agencies did make a decision. By May 1965 all four of them had decided to approve construction of the power plant. They had each come to a decision independently. The Minnesota Conservation Commission and the Minnesota Water Pollution Control Commission had decided that use of the St. Croix water would not be harmful. The Army Corps of Engineers had ruled that to build docking facilities and to allow barge traffic on the river would be safe. The little village of Oak Park Heights had decided that the plant would benefit the community. Finally, the State Health Board had ruled that air pollution would not be dangerous to the area.

Northern States Power Company began construction immediately. At this point the State of Wisconsin took up the battle, eventually taking the case to the U. S. Supreme Court in an attempt to obtain an injunction to halt construction of the plant. However, the court refused to grant an injunction. The Allen S. King plant was to become a reality, and construction continued full speed ahead.

Not all battles for the environment are won. The Save the St. Croix organization lost this one, but the war is being won. The Allen S. King controversy was only the beginning of an awareness on the part of all citizens of what might be called an environmental ethic. An editorial in the *St. Paul Pioneer Press* on February 4, 1965, said:

> The debate over this one power plant has served the useful purpose of focusing attention on this problem, of demonstrating how poorly equipped this state is to meet this challenge in a dispassionate manner that will protect both public and private needs.[10]

This focusing of attention was necessary before citizens, industry, and government could come together and draw up methods by which they could all have some input in environmental decisions. For contrary to what Judge McDonough said, such decisions are too important to be left to the "experts." Again we come down to the fact that it is the citizens, all of us, who must decide whether to protect natural areas in this country such as the St. Croix. Senator Nelson put it best when he said in 1965:

> The fact is that the fight over the location of this plant reveals a gap in the fabric of our institutions. This is a genuine honorable conflict. Which is to come first on the St. Croix—power development or recreation? Who can decide?
>
> This raises the age-old question of land use and resource use, a question that must daily be decided in situation after situation across the country. Whose responsibility is it?[11]

The "gap in our institutions" Senator Nelson referred to involved an absence of laws that both protected the environment and provided the means for citizen input in decision making. The St. Croix power plant controversy helped to trigger a number of reforms, many of them legislative, which would enable a fair and orderly resolution of future conflicts. Some positive results of the conflict were:

- It highlighted the need for federal water pollution control legislation which would enforce interstate cooperation and uniform water quality standards, and would emphasize prevention of any water pollution problems rather than relying on punishment of offenders.
- It demonstrated the inadequacy of governmental systems and procedures in the area of citizen input in decision making.
- It emphasized the need for better regional planning.

• It drew attention of the citizens of Minnesota and Wisconsin to a valuable natural resource, the St. Croix River, and alerted individuals to their responsibilities for protection of that resource.

• It showed that there are some wild areas of the nation that need the protection of federal legislation if they are to remain forever wild.

As we shall see, during the next ten years much progress was made to satisfy many of these needs. Legislation on

The completed Allen S. King power plant. Its smokestack can be seen for miles along the river.

state and federal levels and regional and local cooperation combined to make the scene much brighter. It all had to start somewhere. Perhaps we should all thank Northern States Power Company for getting things going.

Today the Allen S. King plant is producing 550,000 kilowatts of power. Several concessions made by NSP have lessened the impact of the plant. For example, cooling towers, not called for initially, were constructed to lower the temperature of the water before returning it to

After the power plant was completed, coal barges started coming up the river to supply it with fuel.

the St. Croix. The barges operate only during daylight hours on weekdays, avoiding the heaviest recreational traffic on the river. And yet the 783-foot smokestack does dominate the valley, visible from miles around as a reminder of industrialization.

In November 1971 NSP announced that it had canceled plans to build the companion power plant on the St. Croix site.

6.

LEGISLATIVE ACTION

The Allen S. King controversy demonstrated the need for more citizen input and participation in environmental decision making, and for increased cooperation between the states of Wisconsin and Minnesota in such decision making. One of the most immediate and significant answers to this need came through legislation in the two states which created a new agency.

The Minnesota-Wisconsin Boundary Area Commission

In an interstate compact in 1965, the two states agreed to cooperate with one another on matters relating to "the present and future protection, use, and development in the public interest, of the lands, river valleys, and waters"

Interstate State Park lies on both sides of the St. Croix River. Both Minnesota and Wisconsin citizens are concerned about the St. Croix's environment, since the river forms the Minnesota-Wisconsin boundary for 127 miles.

which form the common boundary between them. A Boundary Area Commission was created to conduct studies and to make recommendations to both states, primarily for the St. Croix and Mississippi rivers. The commission would also act as a coordinating force for the various communities along the rivers.

The states agreed to consider recommendations of the commission on such matters as regional planning, air and water pollution, water quality and use, erosion, diversion of waters, land-use developments, and preserving the scenic and recreational character of the river basin.

During the past ten years, the commission has done much to increase interstate cooperation and public participation in decisions which affect the St. Croix. It has staged public conferences on regulation of boating use and carrying out the Wild and Scenic Rivers Act, which we shall examine shortly. It has offered advice and information on river planning to local officials. It has issued special information bulletins to over two thousand area residents on such subjects as pending federal legislation, public hearings, and local river problems. It has functioned as a neutral link between federal agencies and the states, and has offered testimony in congressional hearing. Finally, it has sponsored an effort to control land development projects on the lower St. Croix.

Most importantly, the Boundary Area Commission has developed a consciousness among the citizens and states involved of the importance of land- and water-use planning. The agency can almost be considered the voice of the river itself, and it has been a leader in the effort to preserve the basin.

Several pieces of federal legislation passed during the late 1960s and early 1970s were also to have a profound effect on solving the environmental problems of the St. Croix, as well as many other rivers in the United States.

The National Environmental Policy Act of 1969

The National Environmental Policy Act made the U. S. government responsible for surveying the condition of the nation's environment and for coordinating efforts toward improvement in that area. The provision of this law which concerns us is the one that requires the writing of environmental impact statements (EIS).

The federal law states:

> Each Federal agency shall prepare a statement of environmental impact in advance of each major action, recommendation, or report

on legislation that may significantly affect the quality of the human environment. Such actions may include new highway construction, harbor dredging or filling, nuclear power plant construction, large-scale aerial pesticide spraying, river channeling, new jet runways, munitions disposal, bridge construction, and more.

The EIS must be written by the federal agency responsible for granting permits for any particular action.

First a draft statement is written, which is made available to the public and to all interested agencies. Then, after a period of time during which anyone may make comments in writing, or in some cases hold public hearings, a final statement is issued that considers all these comments. An EIS alerts the public and the government to the environmental consequences of a proposed action, so that environmental considerations are always a part of the decision making procedure. It allows for citizen input in any major actions which affect our environment.

A number of states have written their own environmental policy acts to supplement the national one. Minnesota has one that calls for an EIS on any project that may affect the environment, whether or not it requires a permit from a state or federal agency. If 500 citizens sign a petition, that in itself can require an EIS to be written. In general an EIS must include:

- A detailed description of the proposed action
- A discussion of the probable impact of that action on the environment
- Discussion of any adverse environmental effects that cannot be avoided
- Alternatives to the proposed action that might avoid some of the adverse environmental effects

- A discussion of problems and objections raised by other federal, state, and local agencies and organizations or individuals (this last is required in the final statement).

The EIS allows for a systematic approach in planning and decision making that affects our environment. It is a vehicle through which many projects that would have been harmful to the environment have either been halted altogether or amended to eliminate their destructive elements.

How did the environmental impact procedure affect the St. Croix? We have seen how little provision existed for public input during the Allen S. King conflict, and how little accountability the power company and the government agencies involved had to the public. Suddenly, with the National Environmental Policy Act, there was a legal mechanism through which the people could be heard in environmental decisions. During the first years since the act was passed, a number of EIS's have been written relating to the river. For example, the U. S. Army Corps of Engineers has written one on their dredging operations, which keep a nine-foot channel open for barge traffic. Statements were written for both the upper and lower St. Croix to make them a part of the Wild and Scenic Rivers System. In all of these, the public has had the opportunity to read about planned actions and to issue comments on and objections to the projects. The prospect of writing an EIS and going through the review system involved has already discouraged some projects that would have been harmful to the St. Croix's environment.

The Federal Water Pollution Control Act Amendments of 1972

The first federal legislation dealing with water pollution was passed in 1948, and some other minor legislation was to follow during the late 1950s and 60s. However, the 1972 amendments to the Federal Water Pollution Control Act of 1965 were without question the most far-reaching water quality legislation ever passed by the U. S. Congress. The new law was very strict, extremely complicated, and costly. In fact, it was passed over the veto of President Nixon, who said it was far too expensive. Recognizing its importance to the nation, an overwhelming majority of Congress voted for the law. In supporting it Congress acknowledged the public pressures exerted by citizens all over the United States, who were demanding that the pollution of the nation's waters be brought to a halt. The 1972 Amendments were the first all-out national attack on water pollution. As we have seen, only a consistent approach for all fifty states could really hope to accomplish the goal of clean water in this country. The goal of the 1972 Amendments is clean water by 1985, and a schedule was set up to achieve it. Rather than concentrating on punishment of polluters, the new law focused on prevention of pollution to begin with. The law had several important features:

- It earmarked enormous amounts of money for its implementation. For example, $18 billion over the first three years alone would be given to aid cities and towns in improving wastewater facilities.
- It established a national permit program aimed at restricting pollutant discharges, whether they were from industries, cities and towns, or large agricul-

tural operations. In the past pollution was judged by measuring the water quality of rivers or lakes. In the future the effluent itself would be measured before it was dumped into the water, which would insure compliance from each individual source of dumping to one set standard.

- It expanded water quality standards programs so that they covered intrastate as well as interstate waters.
- It provided mechanisms for citizen participation in carrying out and enforcing the law. Public educational meetings were to be held. In many cases, public hearings are required before important agency decisions can be made. The public is invited to participate in writing regulations, setting standards, and water-use planning. Reports are to be made to the public on significant agency decisions. Furthermore, provision was made for citizen suits against *either* a polluter *or* state or federal agencies which failed to enforce standards of water quality.
- Penalties for violation of the new law were much stricter than any previous pollution penalties.

No one expected the waters of the nation to be cleaned up overnight once this bill was passed. However, the law created a new system of federal control over water quality which should help all of us to move toward the goal of clean water, if not by 1985, at least by the end of the century. Like so many kinds of pollution, it is possible to eliminate it *if* we are willing to pay the bill and to closely watch our progress. Citizens must all participate in this battle. As the Izaak Walton League has put it, "Clean water? It's still up to you—now you must be up to it!"

What did this law mean for the St. Croix? It was an

enforcement tool which both state and local governments could use to upgrade water quality. In February 1973 the Wisconsin Department of Natural Resources issued thirty-six orders to end water pollution, including twenty-four against communities with inadequate sewage treatment systems and twelve against industries whose wastes are emptied into the St. Croix and its tributaries. The order stated that it was backed by the 1972 water quality legislation. The State of Wisconsin knew that under this law these communities could apply for federal aid for improvements and that industries involved could get stiff penalties if they did not cooperate. While water pollution has not become a major problem for the St. Croix, the federal legislation was to serve as insurance against such a thing ever happening.

7.

VOICES OF THE PEOPLE

On October 2, 1968, Congress passed by a large majority the Wild and Scenic Rivers Act, which declared that:

> Certain selected rivers of the Nation, which, with their immediate environments, possess outstandingly remarkable scenic, recreational, geologic, fish and wild life, historic, cultural, or other similar values, shall be preserved in free-flowing condition, and that they and their immediate environments shall be protected for the benefit and enjoyment of present and future generations.

This law gave immediate wild river status to all or portions of eight rivers in the United States, including the upper St. Croix, and designated twenty-seven other rivers for detailed study as potential additions to the national system. In addition to the upper St. Croix, the act gave wild river status to the following rivers: the Rio Grande in New Mexico and the Wolf in Wisconsin, to be administered by the Interior Department; the Eleven Point in Missouri, the Middle Fork of the Feather in California, the Middle Fork of the Clearwater and the Middle Fork of the Salmon in Idaho, to be administered by the Department of Agriculture; and the Rogue in Oregon, to be administered jointly by both departments. In a joint statement, the Secretaries of the Interior and Agriculture said:

> America's rivers flow deep through our national consciousness. Their courses beckoned us to explore a new continent and to build a Nation, and we have come to know, depend upon, and love the rivers that water our land.
>
> We have harnessed many of our rivers, dedicating some to navigation, others to power, water supply and disposal of wastes. But we have not yet made stock of our rivers as we first knew them: wild and free-flowing. In a Nation as bountifully endowed with rivers as ours, it is time to do so.[12]

Inclusion in the Wild and Scenic Rivers System involves classification of each river in one of three categories:

- Wild River Areas—"are free of impoundments, and generally inaccessible except by trail, with watersheds or shorelines essentially primitive and waters unpolluted."
- Scenic River Areas—"are free of impoundments, with shorelines or watersheds still largely primitive and shorelines largely undeveloped, but accessible in places by roads."
- Recreational River Areas—"are readily accessible by road or railroad, may have some development along their shorelines, and may have undergone some impoundment or diversion in the past."

The Wild and Scenic Rivers Act affords special protection from development to the rivers in the system. A five-year ban on development was established for the rivers under consideration as part of the system, so that they, too, would be given the same protection. The law also provides for acquiring certain portions of the land along the Wild and Scenic Rivers by either state or federal governments, depending on which one will administer the river. Land remaining under private ownership falls under river-wide zoning laws that enforce land use in agreement with the basic intent of the act, to preserve and protect the river.

The new legislation radically affected the St. Croix. In 1968 the upper portion of the river was made a part of the original system. This was made possible by an enormous gift of land along its banks, which had been owned for years by NSP. The lower fifty-two miles however, were included only after much debate and negotiation in Washington. It took the help of countless citizens who wrote letters and offered testimony, and the support of the members of Congress from the two states. The main stumbling block seemed to be that the lower St. Croix was more developed. The U. S. Department of the Interior questioned whether it was appropriate to include such a developed area in the system, but the dedication of many individuals finally persuaded the government.

Testimony was taken by Congressional committee in St. Croix Falls, Wisconsin, in October 1971, and in Washington, D.C., in April 1972 on legislation to include the lower St. Croix in the Wild and Scenic Rivers System. Let's listen to what some of these people said.

Don Iverson, Hudson, Wisconsin, representing St. Croix County

I come here today as a resident of the St. Croix River Valley for the past forty-five years, born and raised here at St. Croix Falls,

Divers try their skill and courage from cliffs along the lower St. Croix. This area is a favorite place for swimming, picnicking, and canoeing. Many people wanted the lower St. Croix to be protected by inclusion in the Wild and Scenic River System.

Other areas of the river are more primitive. The upper portion of the St. Croix was made part of the Wild and Scenic River System in 1968 because of the lack of development along its shores.

and as the father of three children. I have watched and listened as the multitude of governmental units along the river have debated its fate. I have watched as hundreds and thousands of people, from Wisconsin and Minnesota, have discovered its fine recreational potential, and swarmed to its waters on weekends. I have watched industry choose the St. Croix as a good site for development because of the water's ability to carry away waste. I have watched residential developers and individuals buy up riverfront property as prime home locations.

It has become pretty obvious to me that the time has come to make some basic decisions about the St. Croix, that we don't have any more time to sit and watch . . . When the lumber companies first came to northern Wisconsin, they really thought they would never run out of those lovely, tall, thick pines. But they did. And we are going to run out of scenic rivers just as surely as they ran out of pines, unless we safeguard them for future generations.[13]

Jonathan P. Ela, Midwest Representative, Sierra Club

The Mississippi River that Mark Twain described in Huck Finn would not even at that time have qualified as a Wild River by today's standards. Much of the river that Huck floated along would not have even made the grade as a Scenic River, falling only in the lowly category of a Recreational River. Yet Huck's trip down the Mississippi has stirred up more romantic blood in more generations of Americans than any other work of American literature. Who among us has not dreamed of duplicating Huck's raft trip?

But today that is an idle dream. Today much of the Mississippi River is so dammed, so leveed, so dredged, so polluted, so busy, so developed and so exploited that a canoe trip through the great sewers of Istanbul might hold equal interest and greater charm.

The lower St. Croix could go the way the lower Mississippi did, but it need not. It can remain, with the passage of S. 1928, a haven for modern Huck Finns, making up in its beauty and diversity for what it lacks in length. It should be one of a large number of protected rivers in the Midwest, for the recreational potential of such a system cannot be overstressed.[14]

Dr. Patrick Nolan, National Representative, Sierra Club

. . . It has been objected that the lower river is already partially

The St. Croix River flows peacefully at St. Croix State Park. Areas like this are protected by the Wild and Scenic Rivers System.

developed, and only the upper river contains enough outstanding scenery to deserve protection. The limited development along the lower St. Croix should not deter action on this bill: we have long passed the time when we can afford the luxury of sacrificing a splendid resource on the pretext that an even more splendid resource exists elsewhere.[15]

Although most witnesses testified in favor of including the lower St. Croix in the Wild and Scenic Rivers System, there were those who opposed it.

Mrs. Karen Hubbard, Lakeland, Minnesota

I have lived along the St. Croix for many years, and my husband has lived along the river for over thirty-five years. It is my opinion that there is no need for such a bill and that such a bill would probably do more harm for the river than good. The proper way to control the river is through local or cooperative state codes or ordinances.

There has been a lot of talk about a master plan. I think the adoption of the so-called master plan would be very inadvisable. It is better to have local initiative, creativiy and development. If you take a look up and down the St. Croix River, you will find it is very well protected and very well developed . . .

The river already is developed to a point where there are no longer these so-called natural values to preserve that would require a federal law or even a state law. The river is built up: it is residential; it is commercial; and it is recreational.[16]

Senator (now Vice President) Walter F. Mondale, Minnesota, claimed that "economic blackmail" had been used to pressure individual communities "into relaxing standards for the protection of treasured natural resources." Speaking about the lower St. Croix, Senator Mondale said it was very difficult to get the cooperation of thirty-seven local governments on land-use and planning issues, and that a mistake by any one local government could endanger the efforts of all the others. Often in the past communities have decided to relax standards in order to attract tax-paying industries, said Mondale. Although no St. Croix Valley community wants this to happen, he said, it would take new federal legislation to save the St. Croix from future environmental destruction.

A long statement opposing the bill was submitted by the Calder Corporation, a development company. Because the state and local governments of Minnesota and Wis-

Vice President Walter Mondale (above), a senator from Minnesota at the time congressional hearings were held on the lower St. Croix, and Senator Gaylord Nelson (below) of Wisconsin cosponsored the bill to include the lower St. Croix in the Wild and Scenic River System. Senator Nelson had introduced bills in 1965 and 1967 to make the upper St. Croix part of the system.

consin could cope with their land-use problems, there was no need for new federal legislation, according to the company. It claimed that recreational use of the St. Croix caused more environmental destruction than "proper" housing development. The Calder Corporation also said that federal legislation could be justified only in cases where development threatened "the health and safety of the people." In its opinion, no such threatening development existed on the St. Croix. It stated that "intelligent developers under modern planning methods would adequately protect the river . . . and thereby do the most good for the most number of people."

After considering the testimony taken in St. Croix Falls and in Washington, D.C., Congress included the lower St. Croix in the Wild and Scenic Rivers System in an act passed in October 1972. Various portions of both the upper and lower river were to have designations of either scenic or recreational, and the lowest twenty-five miles would be administered by the two states, with the rest under the federal government. The next step was the writing of master plans for the upper and lower sections of the river. These plans were to deal with the purposes of the river, its resource values, its relationship to the region, its management objectives, and the overall concepts of land acquisition, land management, and any development which might take place. Citizens and local units of government as well as state and federal officials worked long, hard hours to provide the input for writing these statements. They could truly be called products of the people on the river—what they wanted to see in the future of the St. Croix.

8.

THE CALDER CONDOMINIUMS

While the Wild and Scenic Rivers Act was being discussed and debated in relation to the St. Croix, a new conflict was brewing on the Wisconsin side of the river. In early 1973 the Calder Corporation of St. Paul, Minnesota had nearly completed plans to build an enormous $75 million housing complex on the bluffs overlooking the river at Hudson, Wisconsin. The initial construction would consist of sixteen luxury condominium units selling at $85,000 each, which would be built into the sloping river banks. As many as 1,500 units would eventually be constructed over a period of several years. The complex would obviously have a great impact on the valley, because it would affect traffic patterns, river use, sewage disposal, school systems, and certainly the beauty of this particularly lovely stretch of the river where no visible major development had existed before.

Mont Croix, as it would be called, would house about thirty-five hundred people and would include some high-rise buildings. The project would obviously enlarge the tax base of Hudson, whose population was about fifty-seven hundred. The city council was impressed, as were many, but not all, of Hudson's residents. Other citizens of the valley were less enthusiastic. Sound familiar? Only a few years ago Oak Park Heights had jumped at the chance to enlarge *its* tax base, over the objections of many St. Croix residents including many citizens of Hudson. In fact, the Hudson city council had been among those against the plant's construction! Values can change when you start talking about your own backyard. But much had changed since 1965. The three major federal laws we discussed were a large part of that change.

The National Environmental Policy Act and state laws provided the machinery to require an Environmental Impact Statement from the Calder Corporation. Such a process could hold up the project for a year or two while the citizens had a chance to examine it closely and to object if they saw fit.

The water quality legislation of 1972 insured that if the project were built, adequate sewage facilities would be provided. The town of Hudson, which was already under pressure to upgrade its sewage system, might now have an additional burden. Although the water quality laws would not stop the project, they would see to it that minimal environmental damage to the river would result from the complex.

The Wild and Scenic Rivers Act was to have the greatest impact on the Calder project. Just as the plans were being finalized between the corporation and the town of Hudson, the states of Minnesota and Wisconsin were racing to finish a Lower St. Croix River Master Plan. Completion of the plan would signal full "membership" of the lower river in the Wild and Scenic Rivers System, and thus automatic restriction, if not elimination, of Mont Croix.

By April 1973 all but one local government unit on the lower portion of the river had agreed to delay any new building permits or land development for six months while the master plan was being written. What community voted against these actions? You guessed it. Hudson felt they were excessively restrictive. Since the Calder project had been in the planning stages since 1971, they felt that they had the right to go ahead. Over the objections of many, including the governors of Minnesota and Wisconsin and the executive director of the Boundary Area Commission, the Hudson City Council in May 1973 gave the project the final go-ahead by a three to two vote.

Communities facing the development site on the Minnesota side of the river immediately threatened to sue, and by July the State of Minnesota had filed suit to stop the development completely or at least delay it until completion of the master plan. The governor of Minnesota threatened to invoke that state's 1973 Land Sales Registration Act that made it illegal to advertise land sales on any site where building was environmentally harmful. Since most purchasers of the new condominiums would probably come from the nearby cities of Minnesota, this would have seriously hampered the project.

On September 27, 1973, the Calder Corporation announced that after negotiations with Minnesota and Wisconsin, they had agreed not to build the sixteen terrace units and would hold off on other developments. The decision of the Calder Corporation was influenced by the "threat" of a required environmental impact statement, the hostility of neighboring communities and states, and the likelihood of lengthy legal battles. Inclusion of the river in the Wild and Scenic Rivers System was the last straw, and the corporation recognized wisely that there was no point in beginning what would probably be a losing battle. As of spring 1977, no construction had begun on this property.

The master plan is now complete, an environmental impact statement has been issued on it, and final provisions are being made in the area of local zoning to include the St. Croix in the system. This story offers hope that future decision making in the valley will be done in a cautious, responsible manner.

9.

RIVER BASIN PLANNING

How do you plan intelligently for the future of a river basin? If the boundaries of a river basin conformed to political boundaries, planning would be easy, or at least more convenient. However, as we have seen with the St. Croix, all kinds of overlapping governmental units usually have some authority over a river basin. So the first requirement for successful and effective planning is cooperation between these groups and all the individuals they represent. We have seen evidence in the past ten years that such cooperation is developing on the St. Croix, thanks to the dedication of many individuals who love the river and are concerned about its future.

Assuming the cooperation is there, where do you begin? The League of Women Voters, in a pamphlet entitled

"Know Your River Basin," suggests you begin with a study of the area. You should ask such questions as:

- What are the characteristics of the river basin?
- What are the water-use and control programs?
- What are the administrative organizations in the river basin?
- What are the major conflicts among users and uses?
- What is the future of the basin?

They go on to suggest that you find out about land ownership, values, and use. For example, you should find out if the area is primarily a bedroom community with the population commuting elsewhere to jobs. You should also know what industries, business, and commercial ventures exist, and how much agriculture there is.

In answering these questions we begin to come up with a profile of the river basin. Other kinds of questions come to mind. For example, what is the history of the area, and how can we learn from past mistakes? What about the more scientific aspects of the region such as hydrology, vegetation, slopes, soils, water tables, and habitat areas? All of these considerations are important if we are to base planning for the future on a realistic and accurate concept of the basin.

Land use planning also involves a discussion of values. Participants must discuss priorities to establish what is important for the area. Some people feel that environmental factors are most important, while others place recreation first on the list. Still others feel that the economy deserves the highest consideration. For this reason it is important that people from many varied groups and interests participate in land-use planning. This means you! The concept of such planning is just beginning to take hold on a large scale in the United States, and now

Fishing from a houseboat on Lake St. Croix. Recreational uses of a river are one factor that must be considered in river basin planning.

is the time to get involved.

It is important, too, that experts, particularly scientific experts, be consulted in planning for the future of a river basin. Because there are laws of nature, certain environmental realities are not open to negotiation. In a sense nature must be there at the bargaining table. The basin and the river must be respected and learned from, and not considered a tool to use for our own ends.

On the other hand, river basin planning may involve some major changes of the river. The extent to which people alter a river depends on its location, physical description, and goals of the planners. Planning may involve irrigation, flood control, navigation, hydroelectric power, water supply, pollution control, recreation, conservation of natural areas, fish, and wildlife. Each of these objectives must be considered in light of what we have learned from our study of the basin. Thus planning becomes quite complicated and requires time and steady, informed input from the planners.

As those involved study, learn, and debate, they begin to see major decisions that must be made. How can we best preserve water quality of this river? Should we limit development or recreational use of the river, and if so, how? What about industry—should it be allowed and under what conditions? How can we insure cooperation of communities in the basin? What can we do to maintain the historical character of the river? How do existing laws fit in with our planning, and what new legislation is needed?

Planning for the St. Croix has been done during the past ten years by several different groups and agencies. The admission of the river in the Wild and Scenic Rivers System in 1968 caused a strong push to map out its future. Now the various communities along the river are in the process of approving a standard set of zoning guidelines. The planning process was successful because so many people along the river were determined that it would be.

On the upper St. Croix planners concentrated on improving and maintaining such programs as wildlife, fish, recreation, forestry, and historical management. They

State park naturalist Lucy Seaver leads a canoe caravan on the St. Croix River.

also dealt with wild land acquisition for the Wild and Scenic Rivers System. Development of primitive campsites, picnic areas, family campgrounds, hiking and snowshoe trails, swimming beaches, scenic road development, boat accesses, and wildlife habitats were all included.

On the lower St. Croix planners had to deal with more complex issues. They considered development and construction on the river banks, limitation of marinas, maintenance of air and water quality, construction of new bridges, adoption of uniform boat toilet and boat safety regulations, sewage treatment programs, and the recreational capacity of the river. The resulting master plans were substantial beginnings, but not the final word. Right now, for example, work is being done to limit and regulate speedboats on the river. More laws need to be passed and more discussions and public hearings should be held. Planning is a neverending process.

However, the basic concept of protection and preservation of the St. Croix for future generations of Americans has become the very foundation for decision making. The citizens have seen to it that their river will be closely guarded and loved and treated with the respect it deserves.

NOTES

1. Grace Lee Nute, *The Voyageur* (St. Paul: Minnesota Historical Society, 1955), p. 14.
2. John Murray Gibbon, *Canadian Folk Songs, Old and New* (New York: E. P. Dutton & Co., 1927).
3. *Gopher Reader,* ed. by A. Mermina Poatgieter and James Taylor Dunn (St. Paul: Minnesota Historical Society, 1958), p. 236.
4. Ibid., p. 196.
5. United States Senate, Committee on Public Works, *Hearings,* December 10 and 11, 1964, Stillwater, Minn. (Washington: Govt. Printing Office, 1965), p. 167.
6. *World Book Encyclopedia* (Chicago: Field Enterprises, 1973) V. 21, p. 92.
7. *Life Magazine,* July 31, 1964.
8. Minnesota Department of Natural Resources and Minnesota Water Pollution Control Commission, *Hearings,* January 14, 1965.
9. *Stillwater Gazette,* January 18, 1965.
10. *St. Paul Pioneer Press,* February 4, 1965.
11. Minnesota DNR *Hearings,* January 14, 1965.
12. United States Department of the Interior, Bureau of Outdoor Recreation and United States Department of Agriculture, Forest Service, *Wild and Scenic Rivers: Authorized by the Wild and Scenic Rivers Act* (Washington: Govt. Printing Office, 1973).
13. United States Senate, Committee on Interior and Insular Affairs, Subcommittee on Public Lands, *Hearings,* October 23, 1972 and April 14, 1972, p. 30.
14. Ibid., p. 37.
15. Ibid., p. 38.
16. Ibid., p. 157.

GLOSSARY

aeration—the process of exposing water to air, either by dividing the water into small drops or by forcing air through the water

deciduous—a term for plants that shed their leaves each year

ecology—the study of living things in relation to their environment

effluent—the outflow of any substance (usually, a waste product) into the environment

eutrophication—the process of fertilizing a body of water by nutrients that produce more organic matter than the self-purification process can use

fault—a fracture in soil or in a rock mass along which movement has occurred, causing one side to be displaced in relation to another. Many earthquakes are caused by slippage along a fault

flood plain—the area along a river where periodic flooding occurs

gradient—the amount a river falls within a given distance

habitat—the natural environment of a plant or animal

hydrological cycle—the process by which water constantly circulates from the sea to the atmosphere to the earth and back to the sea again

hydrology—a science dealing with the properties, distribution, and circulation of water on the surface of the land, in the soil and underlying rocks, and in the atmosphere

impoundment—a body of water formed by collecting or confining water in or as if in a reservoir

nutrient—a substance that produces growth of organic matter

oxidation—the process of combining water with oxygen

oxidation treatment—the process of exposing waste water to oxygen, which allows the organisms present in the oxygen to convert sewage to clean water photosynthesis—the process by which sugar is manufactured in green plants. It requires carbon dioxide, water, light, and chlorophyll

pollutant—a substance (usually a waste product) produced by human beings that contaminates the natural environment

precipitation—the discharge of condensed water vapor by the atmosphere in the form of rain, hail, sleet, or snow

thermal pollution—the ejection of heated water into the environment, usually into a river, lake, or ocean, raising the temperature above normal limits

transpiration—the evaporation of water from the surface of plants (usually from the leaves) exposed to the air. A large portion of the water the roots take in is eventually lost to the air

tributary—a stream or other body of water that contributes its water to a larger body of water

watershed—the total surface drainage area that contributes water to a river, stream, or lake

BIBLIOGRAPHY

Dunn, James Taylor. *The St. Croix: Midwest Border River.* New York: Holt, Rinehart, and Winston, 1965.

This is the definitive history of the St. Croix, full of interesting material on the past of the river. It provides a particularly good description of the lumber era.

Leopold, Luna B., Davis, Kenneth S., and the Editors of Time-Life Books. *Water.* New York: Time-Life Books, 1966.

A very graphic book on all facets of water. This book has excellent, vivid descriptions of water, the hydrological cycle, chemistry, geology, etc.

Migel, J. Michael, editor, *The Stream Conservation Handbook.* New York: Crown Publishing Company, 1974.

This is an outstanding book, written by and for those who fish but of interest to all of us. Chapters on life in a stream, what kills streams, how to improve them, what groups and individuals can do politically and even legally to preserve and protect rivers. An excellent citizen-action primer for us all—with lots of good scientific background.

Perry, John and Jane Greverus. *Exploring the River.* New York: McGraw Hill, 1960.

This book describes the exploration of a river by a young person, discusses floods, food chains, pollution, water systems, watersheds, etc. Clear explanations are helpful to adults as well as younger readers.

Pringle, Laurence. *This is a River: Exploring an Ecosystem.* New York: MacMillan, 1972.

Pringle, Laurence. *Wild River*. Philadelphia: J. B. Lippincott, Co., no date.

A visually beautiful book with an intelligent text as well. Photos of artistic quality of wild rivers of the United States, and a discussion of their value and preservation.

Usinger, Robert L. *The Life of Rivers and Streams*. New York: McGraw Hill in cooperation with the World Book Encyclopedia, 1967.

Beautifully illustrated, well written. Covers all river life, extensive discussion of how water systems work and of pollution. Good section on how to study fresh water life, and an excellent bibliography.

THE AUTHOR

Wendy Wriston Adamson earned a bachelor's degree in political science from Syracuse University in 1964, and a master's degree in library science from Simmons College in 1971. The following year she helped set up and staff the Environmental Conservation Library within the Minneapolis Public Library. From 1972 to 1974, Ms. Adamson was a librarian at the Environmental Library of Minnesota. She is the author of *Saving Lake Superior* and has recently co-authored a book on solar energy. She and her husband have two children and live in Minneapolis.